100 facts
VOLCANOES

100 facts
VOLCANOES

Chris Oxlade

Consultant: John Farndon

Miles
Kelly

First published in 2009 by Miles Kelly Publishing Ltd
Harding's Barn, Bardfield End Green, Thaxted, Essex, CM6 3PX

This edition printed 2016

6 8 10 9 7

Publishing Director Belinda Gallagher
Creative Director   Jo Cowan
Assistant Editor Carly Blake
Volume Designer Sally Lace
Image Manager Lorraine King
Indexer Jane Parker
Production Elizabeth Collins, Caroline Kelly
Reprographics Stephan Davis, Jennifer Cozens, Thom Allaway
Assets Lorraine King

ISBN 978-1-78617-171-9

Printed in China

British Library Cataloging-in-Publication Data
A catalog record for this book is available from the British Library

ACKNOWLEDGMENTS
The publishers would like to thank the following artists
who have contributed to this book:

Mike Foster, Mike Saunders, Mike White

All other artwork from the Miles Kelly Artwork Bank

The publishers would like to thank the following
sources for the use of their photographs:

Cover KRAFFT/HOA-QUI/Science Photo Library
Page 6 Goodshoot/Photolibrary; 10 Yann Arthus-Bertrand/Corbis; 11 NASA; 19(t) Jean du Boisberranger/Hemis/Corbis;
20 Douglas Peebles/Corbis; 21 Bettmann/Corbis; 23 Marko Heuver/Fotolia.com; 24 Bernhard Edmaier/Science Photo Library;
25(t) Michael S. Yamashita/Corbis, (b) James Andanson/Sygma/Corbis; 26 AFP/Getty Images; 27 Jacques Langevin/Corbis Sygma;
28-29 Philippe Bourseiller/Getty Images; 29 AFP/Getty Images; 30(b) NASA/Carnegie Mellon University/Science Photo Library;
31 Philippe Bourseiller/Getty Images; 32 S Jonasson/FLPA; 33(t) Vittoriano Rastelli/Corbis, (b) Roger Ressmeyer/Corbis;
34 Bettmann/Corbis, (b) Austin Post, Glaciology/U.S. Geological Survey; 35(t) GeoEye satellite image; 36 Alberto Garcia/Corbis;
37(t) Sipa Press/Rex Features, (b) Corbis; 39 Bettmann/Corbis; 40 GeoEye satellite image, (b) Fredrik Fransson; 41(t) Jacques Descloitres/
MODIS Rapid Response Project at NASA/GSFC, (b) Fredrik Fransson; 43(t) TAKE 27 LTD/Science Photo Library, (b) NASA/Science
Photo Library; 44 Jonathan S. Blair/National Geographic/Getty Images; 45 NASA Jet Propulsion Laboratory (NASA-JPL);
46 R.CREATION/amanaimages/Corbis

All other photographs are from:

Corel, digitalSTOCK, digitalvision, iStockphoto.com, John Foxx, PhotoAlto,
PhotoDisc, PhotoEssentials, PhotoPro, Stockbyte

Every effort has been made to acknowledge the source and copyright holder of each picture.
Miles Kelly Publishing apologizes for any unintentional errors or omissions.

Made with paper from a sustainable forest

www.mileskelly.net

Contents

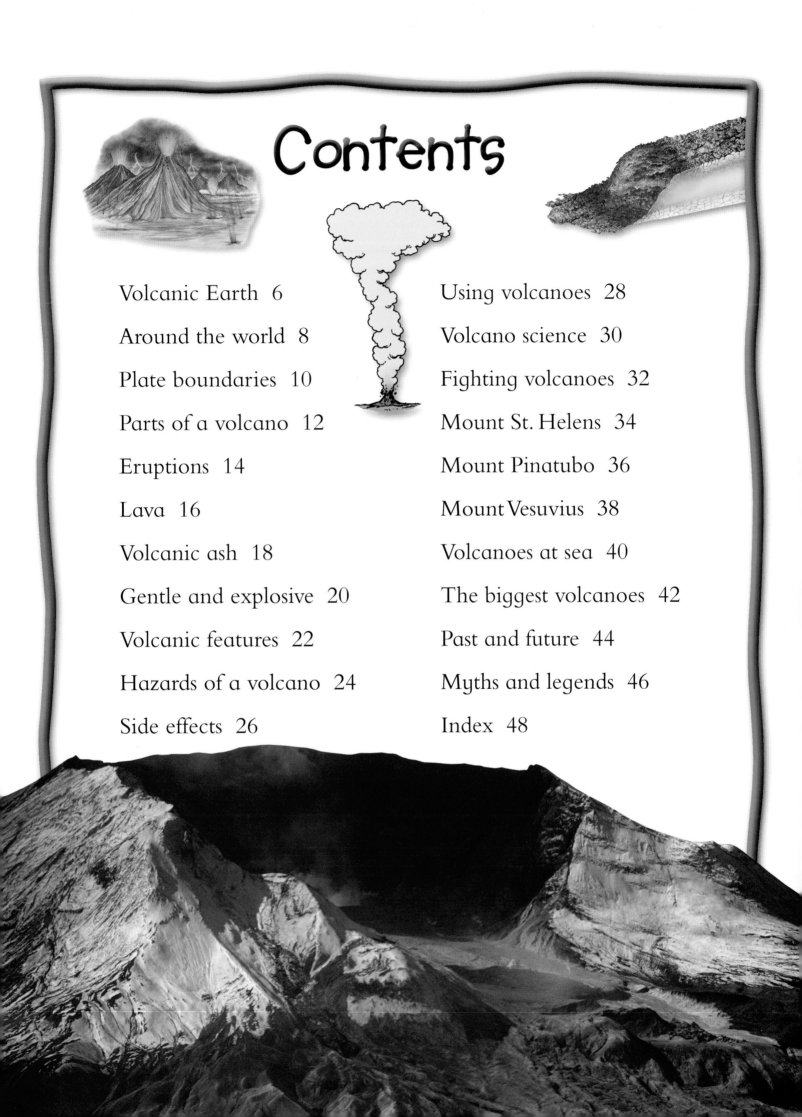

Volcanic Earth

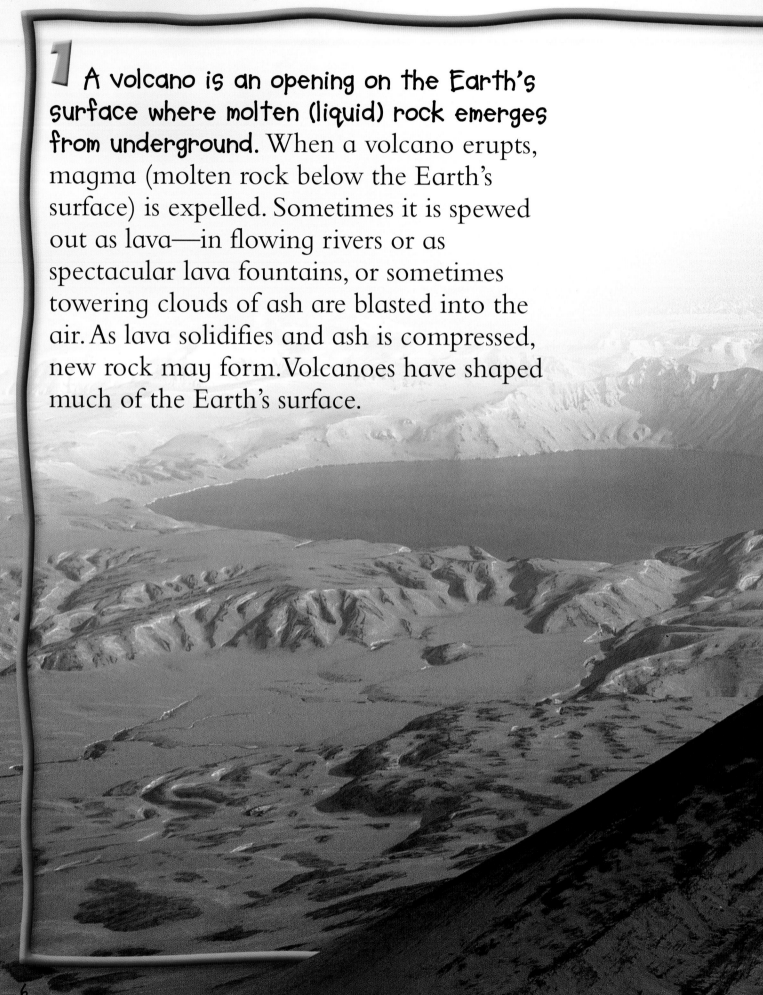

1 A volcano is an opening on the Earth's surface where molten (liquid) rock emerges from underground. When a volcano erupts, magma (molten rock below the Earth's surface) is expelled. Sometimes it is spewed out as lava—in flowing rivers or as spectacular lava fountains, or sometimes towering clouds of ash are blasted into the air. As lava solidifies and ash is compressed, new rock may form. Volcanoes have shaped much of the Earth's surface.

▼ This is Karymsky, a volcano in eastern Russia. Its perfect cone has been built up from layers of erupted ash and lava.

2 **Volcanoes happen because the Earth is hot inside.** The surface is cool, but it gets hotter the deeper you go into the Earth. Under the crust, magma is under so much pressure that it is almost solid. Sometimes the pressure is released by the shifting of the crust and the magma melts. Then it can bubble up through the cracks in the crust as volcanoes.

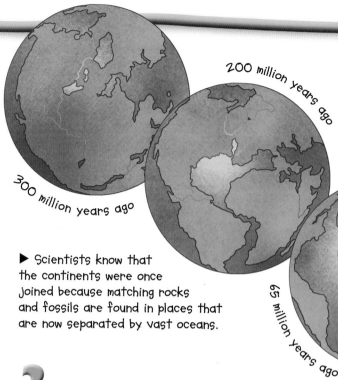

200 million years ago

300 million years ago

65 million years ago

▶ Scientists know that the continents were once joined because matching rocks and fossils are found in places that are now separated by vast oceans.

3 **The Earth's crust is cracked into giant pieces called tectonic plates.** There are about 60 plates, and the seven largest are thousands of miles across. Tectonic plates move slowly across the Earth's surface. This movement, called continental drift, has caused the continents to move apart over millions of years.

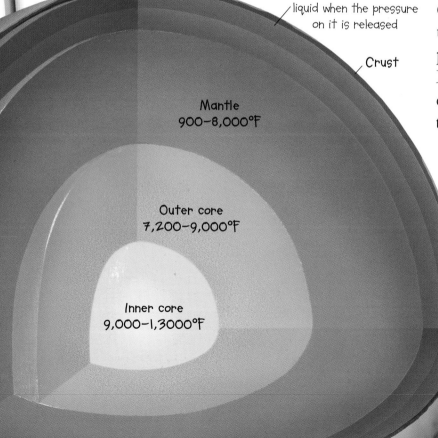

A few miles below the crust, magma becomes liquid when the pressure on it is released

Crust

Mantle
900–8,000°F

Outer core
7,200–9,000°F

Inner core
9,000–1,3000°F

◀ The internal structure of the Earth. The center of the Earth—the inner core—is solid even though it is intensely hot. This is because it is under extreme pressure.

I DON'T BELIEVE IT!
Tectonic plates move at about the same speed as your fingernails grow. That is just an inch or so each year.

4 About 250 million years ago, there was just one continent, known as Pangaea. The movement of tectonic plates broke Pangaea apart and moved the land around to form the continents we recognize today.

5 Most volcanoes erupt along plate boundaries. These are the cracks separating tectonic plates. On a world map of plate boundaries (below) you can see there are often rows of volcanoes along boundaries.

6 Volcanoes also happen at "hot spots." These are places where especially hot magma being driven upward in the mantle burns through the middle of a plate to form volcanoes. The most famous hot-spot volcanoes are those of the Hawaiian islands.

▼ Most active volcanoes occur along the "Ring of Fire" (tinted red). Five volcanoes from around the world are highlighted on the map below.

Hawaii, Pacific Ocean

Mount Rainier, North America

Mount Bromo, Asia

EURASIAN PLATE

RING OF FIRE

NORTH AMERICAN PLATE

AFRICAN PLATE

PACIFIC PLATE

INDO AUSTRALIAN PLATE

SOUTH AMERICAN PLATE

ANTARCTIC PLATE

Arenal, South America

Mount Kilimanjaro, Africa

Plate boundaries

7 **Tectonic plates meet at plate boundaries.** The plates on either side of a boundary are moving at different speeds and in different directions. There are three types of plate boundary: constructive, destructive, and transform.

8 **In some places, tectonic plates move away from each other.** The boundaries between these plates are known as constructive boundaries. As the plates move apart, magma moves up from below into the gap and cools, forming new crust.

▶ At Thingvellir in Iceland, giant cracks in the landscape show the position of a constructive plate boundary.

Plates move apart

Magma erupts through the gap

Mantle

▲ Constructive boundaries often occur in the middle of oceans, forming ocean ridges.

9 **Some volcanoes occur along constructive boundaries.** Most constructive boundaries are under the ocean, so volcanic activity here usually goes unnoticed. The Mid-Atlantic Ridge is an undersea constructive boundary, and the volcanic islands of the Azores, off Portugal, have formed over it.

10 In other places, tectonic plates move toward each other. The boundaries between these plates are called destructive boundaries. One of the plates often dips below the other and is destroyed as it moves into the mantle below. This is called subduction.

▼ Here, an oceanic plate dips below a continental plate. The thinner oceanic plate is pushed down into the mantle.

Plates move together

Subducted plate melts into mantle

A volcano has formed along the edge of the overlying plate

▲ The Aleutian Islands, off Alaska, are volcanic islands, formed along a destructive plate boundary.

11 Some volcanoes form on destructive plate boundaries. As one plate is forced down, magma may force its way up through the plate above. If it melts through the surface, it erupts as a violent volcano. The volcanoes of the Andes, South America, have formed over a subduction zone.

I DON'T BELIEVE IT!
The Mid-Atlantic Ridge stretches 8,700 miles along the sea floor under the Atlantic Ocean.

Parts of a volcano

12 **Material erupted from a volcano can build up to form a mountain.** Beneath the surface is a system of pipes and chambers that supply the volcano with magma from below the crust.

13 A magma chamber is a store of molten rock under a volcano. As magma moves through cracks in the Earth's crust, it collects in huge reservoirs underground. Magma chambers are usually 1–6 miles underground. Some volcanoes have several magma chambers.

14 **Magma rises up through a conduit.** This is a giant pipe that leads from the magma chamber to the surface. Usually there is one main conduit that leads to the summit of a volcano. The hole at the top of the conduit is called a vent. There are often side vents on a volcano's slopes that have branched off the main conduit.

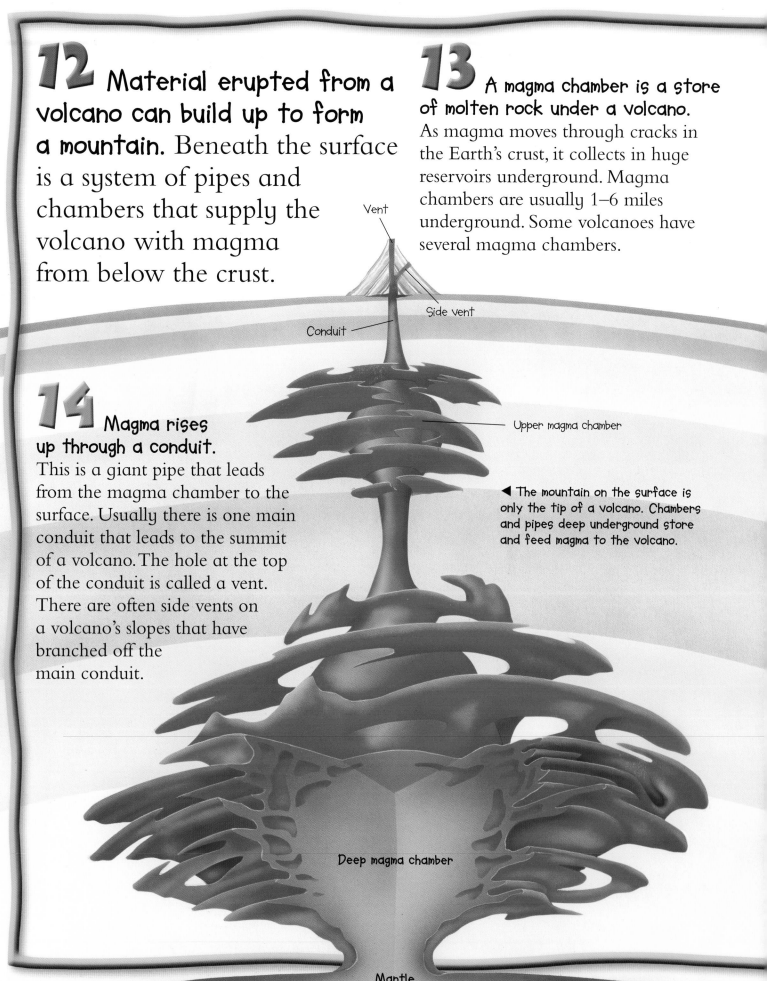

Vent

Side vent

Conduit

Upper magma chamber

◀ The mountain on the surface is only the tip of a volcano. Chambers and pipes deep underground store and feed magma to the volcano.

Deep magma chamber

Mantle

A **composite volcano** (also known as a stratovolcano) has steep sides built up of layers of lava and ash.

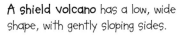

▶ Volcanoes come in different shapes and sizes. Here are three common examples.

A **shield volcano** has a low, wide shape, with gently sloping sides.

A **caldera** is a huge crater left after an old eruption. New cones often grow again inside.

15
A crater can form around the vent of a volcano. As magma is blasted out during an eruption, the material forms a rim around the top of the vent. Sometimes several vents may be erupting into the same crater. A crater can fill with lava during an eruption. When this forms a pool it is known as a lava lake.

▼ Crater Lake, in Oregon, formed in the caldera of Mount Mazama and is around 6 miles across.

16
Lakes can form in the craters of dormant (inactive) volcanoes. When a volcano stops erupting and cools down, its crater can slowly fill with rainwater, creating a lake. Crater lakes also form in calderas— huge craters that form when a volcano collapses into its empty magma chamber.

QUIZ
Which of these are parts of a volcano?
1. Conduit
2. Bed chamber
3. Side vent
4. Ventricle
5. Crater

Answers:
Only 1, 3, and 5 are parts of a volcano

Eruptions

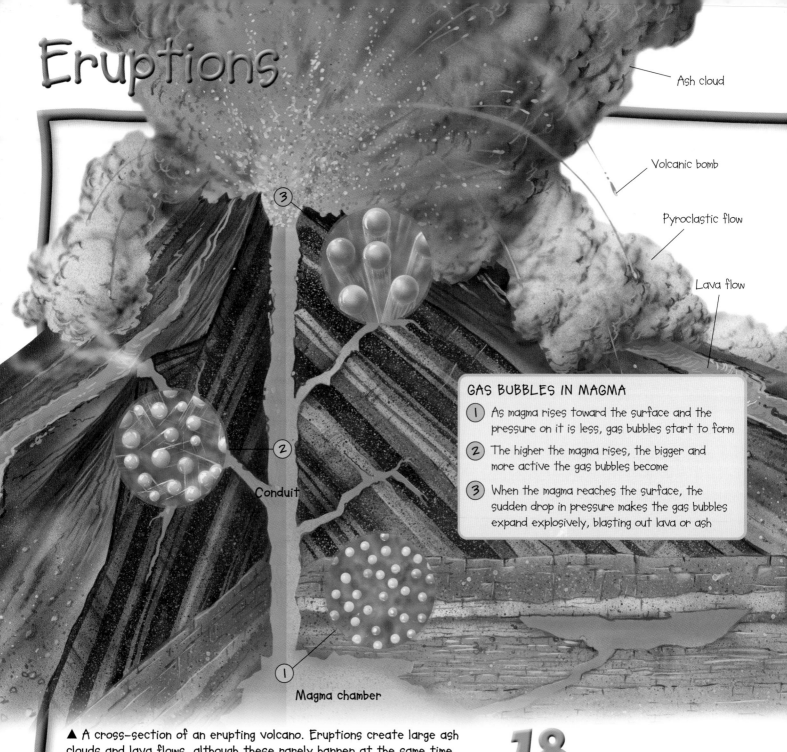

Ash cloud

Volcanic bomb

Pyroclastic flow

Lava flow

③

②

Conduit

GAS BUBBLES IN MAGMA

① As magma rises toward the surface and the pressure on it is less, gas bubbles start to form

② The higher the magma rises, the bigger and more active the gas bubbles become

③ When the magma reaches the surface, the sudden drop in pressure makes the gas bubbles expand explosively, blasting out lava or ash

①

Magma chamber

▲ A cross-section of an erupting volcano. Eruptions create large ash clouds and lava flows, although these rarely happen at the same time.

17 **At any time, about 20 volcanoes are erupting around the world.** On average, 60 volcanoes erupt each year. Eruptions can go on for just a few days or for years on end. A single eruption can spew out millions of tons of material.

18 **An eruption happens when magma swells beneath the Earth's surface.** Magma is a mixture of molten rock and other materials, including dissolved water and gases. As magma rises, the pressure on it lessens. This allows the dissolved gas and water to form bubbles. This makes the magma swell quickly, causing an eruption.

▲ The island of Stromboli, Italy, is an active volcano that erupts almost continuously.

19
As well as lava and hot gases, explosive eruptions throw out pieces of solid magma. As the volcano erupts, the pieces of rock are blasted into billions of fragments called pyroclasts. These fragments mainly form vast clouds of ash during an eruption.

20
A volcano can be active or dormant. An active volcano is one that is erupting now or seems likely to erupt. Some scientists define an active volcano as one that has erupted in the last 10,000 years. A dormant volcano is one that is not active at the moment, but might become so in the future.

21
Volcanoes that seem unlikely to erupt again are described as extinct. Some say that a volcano that has not erupted in the last 10,000 years is extinct. But experts cannot always be sure that a volcano will never erupt again.

▶ Sugar Loaf Mountain in Brazil is a volcanic plug— the solidified core of an extinct volcano.

GASES IN MAGMA

You will need:
bottle of soda

Shake the bottle of soda a little, but not too much, and put it in the sink. As you gradually open the cap, watch the soda in the bottle closely. Bubbles of gas will form, rush upward, and force the soda out of the bottle. The gas stays dissolved in the soda until the pressure on the soda is released. This is the same as what happens when the pressure on magma is released.

Lava

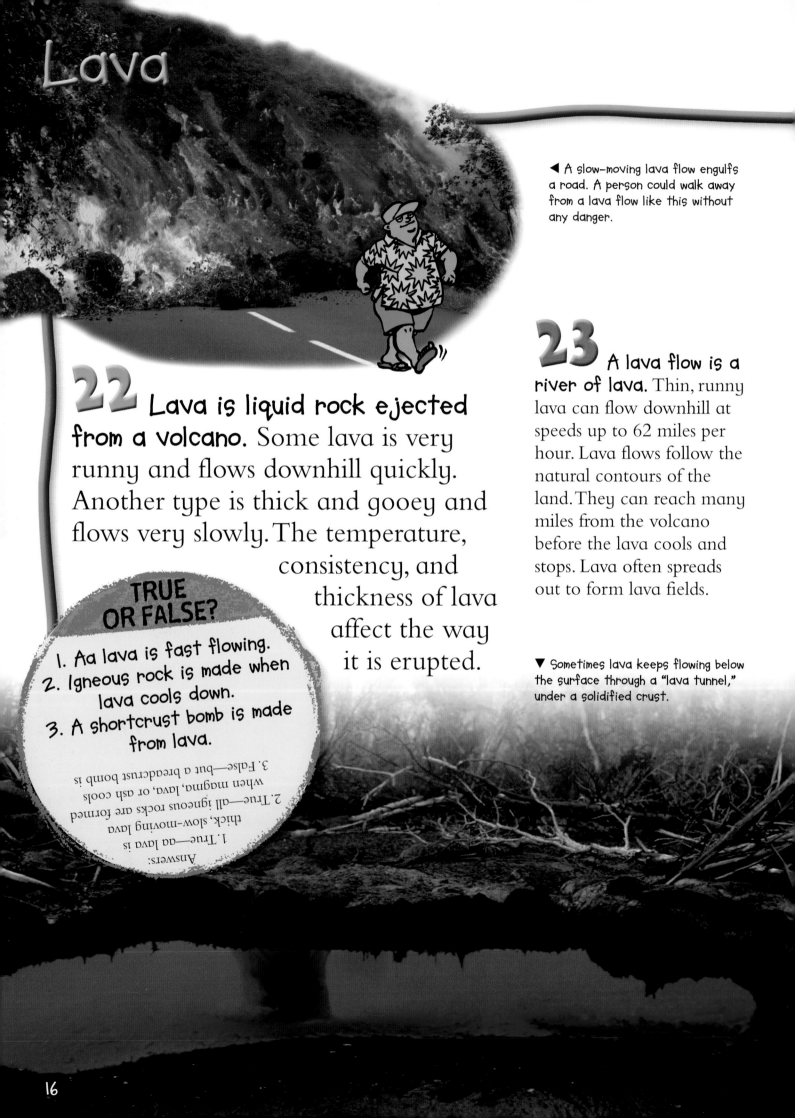

◀ A slow-moving lava flow engulfs a road. A person could walk away from a lava flow like this without any danger.

22 **Lava is liquid rock ejected from a volcano.** Some lava is very runny and flows downhill quickly. Another type is thick and gooey and flows very slowly. The temperature, consistency, and thickness of lava affect the way it is erupted.

23 **A lava flow is a river of lava.** Thin, runny lava can flow downhill at speeds up to 62 miles per hour. Lava flows follow the natural contours of the land. They can reach many miles from the volcano before the lava cools and stops. Lava often spreads out to form lava fields.

▼ Sometimes lava keeps flowing below the surface through a "lava tunnel," under a solidified crust.

TRUE OR FALSE?

1. Aa lava is fast flowing.
2. Igneous rock is made when lava cools down.
3. A shortcrust bomb is made from lava.

Answers:
1. True—aa lava is thick, slow-moving lava
2. True—all igneous rocks are formed when magma, lava, or ash cools
3. False—but a breadcrust bomb is

24 **When lava or magma cools, it forms rock.** This rock is called igneous rock. Basalt—a dark-colored rock—is one common type of igneous rock. Over time, lava flows build up on top of each other forming deep layers of igneous rock.

The front of the lava flow is steep

▲ Slow-flowing lava with a jagged surface is called aa lava.

25 **Pahoehoe and aa are the two main types of lava.** Thick lava that flows slowly cools to form jagged blocks. This is called aa (say "ah") lava. Fast-flowing, runny lava cools to form rock with a smooth surface. This is called pahoehoe (say "pa-hoey-hoey") lava.

Lava has a smooth, folded surface

▲ Fast-flowing lava, called pahoehoe lava, cools to form smooth, rope-like rock.

▶ Pele's tears are tiny lava bombs often produced in Hawaiian eruptions.

Pele's tears

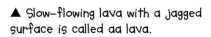

Breadcrust bomb

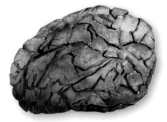

Spindle bomb

Cow pie bomb

Ribbon bomb

26 **A volcanic bomb is a flying lump of lava.** Lumps of lava, usually bigger than the size of a fist, are thrown upward by jets of gas from the vent during an eruption. Sometimes the outside of a bomb solidifies while it is in the air and splits open when it lands. This is called a breadcrust bomb. If the bomb is still soft when it lands, the bomb splats like a cow pie.

◀ Lumps of lava blasted into the air by a volcano form different shapes in the air.

Volcanic ash

27 Volcanic ash is made up of tiny bits of rock. Close up, pieces of ash look like tiny shards of glass. Sometimes, frothy lumps of lava are blasted out with the ash. They cool to form pumice rock, which looks like honeycomb.

▶ Pumice rock is full of holes, making it very light.

28 Towering clouds of ash form during explosive eruptions. Hot gases rush out of a volcano's vent at hundreds of feet a second, firing ash thousands of feet into the air. It billows upward and outward in an eruption column. These towering ash clouds can reach more than 30 miles into the sky.

MAKE A MODEL VOLCANO

You will need:

vinegar plastic bottle baking soda pitcher red food coloring tray sand

Put a tablespoon of baking soda in the bottle. Stand the bottle on a tray and make a cone of sand around it. Put a few drops of red food coloring in half a cup of vinegar. Use the pitcher to pour the vinegar into the bottle. The volcano should erupt with red frothy lava!

▶ Ash is blasted into the sky from the crater of Mount St. Helens.

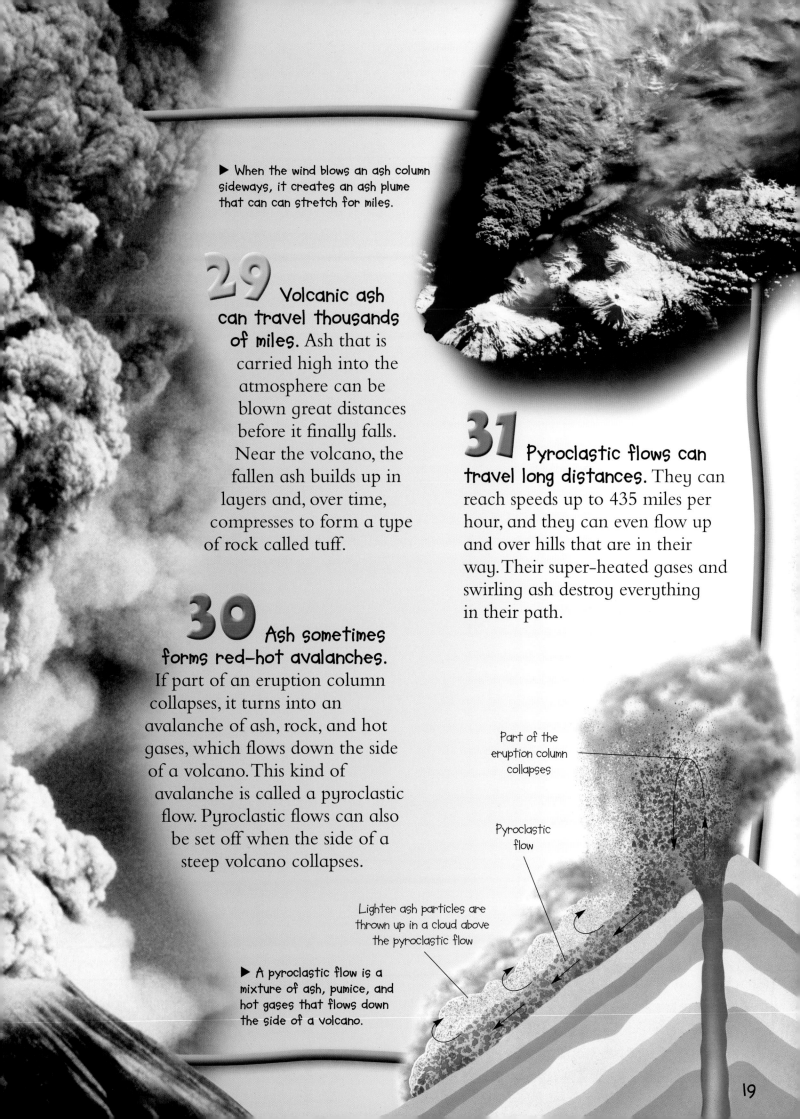

▶ When the wind blows an ash column sideways, it creates an ash plume that can can stretch for miles.

29 **Volcanic ash can travel thousands of miles.** Ash that is carried high into the atmosphere can be blown great distances before it finally falls. Near the volcano, the fallen ash builds up in layers and, over time, compresses to form a type of rock called tuff.

30 **Ash sometimes forms red-hot avalanches.** If part of an eruption column collapses, it turns into an avalanche of ash, rock, and hot gases, which flows down the side of a volcano. This kind of avalanche is called a pyroclastic flow. Pyroclastic flows can also be set off when the side of a steep volcano collapses.

31 **Pyroclastic flows can travel long distances.** They can reach speeds up to 435 miles per hour, and they can even flow up and over hills that are in their way. Their super-heated gases and swirling ash destroy everything in their path.

Part of the eruption column collapses

Pyroclastic flow

Lighter ash particles are thrown up in a cloud above the pyroclastic flow

▶ A pyroclastic flow is a mixture of ash, pumice, and hot gases that flows down the side of a volcano.

Gentle and explosive

32 When you think of an eruption, you probably imagine lava flowing out of a crater. Lava is produced in relatively gentle eruptions. An explosive eruption produces lots of ash and may even blast the mountain apart!

◄ The volcano of Kilauea on Hawaii's Big Island erupts quite gently. Lava fountains like this are common in Hawaiian eruptions.

33 Runny magma produces gentle eruptions. Bubbles of gas rise easily through runny magma and escape from the volcano with little buildup of pressure. So lava flows gently from the volcano's vent. Gentle eruptions occur over hot spots and constructive plate boundaries.

34 Gentle eruptions produce lots of lava. Rivers of lava often flow from side vents as well as the main vent, down the mountainside. If there is a lot of gas in the magma, lava is blasted upward in towering lava fountains.

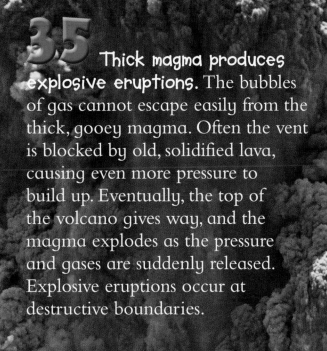

35 **Thick magma produces explosive eruptions.** The bubbles of gas cannot escape easily from the thick, gooey magma. Often the vent is blocked by old, solidified lava, causing even more pressure to build up. Eventually, the top of the volcano gives way, and the magma explodes as the pressure and gases are suddenly released. Explosive eruptions occur at destructive boundaries.

▶ In 1963, Mount Irazu in Costa Rica, South America, erupted explosively. It covered the town of San José, 33.5 miles away, in a thick layer of ash.

36 **Explosive eruptions produce clouds of ash.** In the early stages of an explosive eruption, a volcano can be erupting hundreds of thousands of tons of ash, gases, and pyroclasts per second. Eruption columns grow extremely quickly—they can reach 12 miles into the sky in 30 minutes.

I DON'T BELIEVE IT!

When runny magma erupts from a volcano, it can form fountains of lava nearly 1,000 feet high. That's as high as the Empire State Building in New York!

Volcanic features

37 Volcanic activity creates features on the landscape. The heat in rocks in regions of volcanic activity cause features such as fumaroles, geysers, hot springs, and boiling mud pools. These features can be seen in places where there are no actual volcanoes.

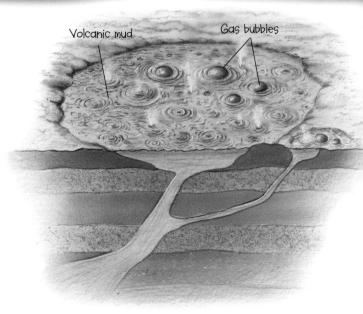

▲ A volcanic mud pool (or mudpot) forms where steam and hot gas bubble up through mud on the surface.

Volcanic mud

Gas bubbles

▼ Iceland's Blue Lagoon geothermal spa. Seawater is heated deep underground, and it emerges as hot springs at the surface, rich in minerals. The nearby geothermal power plant uses the heat to produce electricity.

38 Fumaroles are steaming holes in the ground. They form where groundwater (water under the ground) comes into contact with hot rock or magma and turns to steam. The steam rises through cracks and vents at the surface as a fumarole. Gases, such as sulfur dioxide, are also emitted.

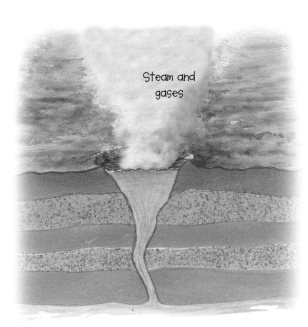

Steam and gases

▲ A fumarole is a hole that emits steam and sulfurous gases. Yellow sulfur crystals often form around the hole.

► Strokkur geyser in Iceland erupts about every five minutes, shooting boiling water and steam about 66 feet into the air.

39 The word "geyser" comes from Iceland. It is derived from the Icelandic word for "gush." The most famous geyser is Old Faithful in Yellowstone National Park. It is called Old Faithful because every hour or so it produces a hot-water fountain 115 feet high.

40 A geyser is a fountain of boiling water and steam. Geysers form when groundwater is heated deep below the ground under pressure. The hot water moves up through rock layers to the surface to find a place to escape. When it starts to bubble up, releasing the pressure, a jet of super-heated water and steam blasts from a hole in the ground for a few seconds.

Hazards of a volcano

41 Volcanic eruptions can be extremely dangerous to anyone living in their vicinity. The main hazards are lava flows, pyroclastic flows, ash, and side effects such as mudflows. In the past, volcanoes have killed thousands of people, destroying homes and even whole villages and towns.

42 Lava flows are very destructive. They can knock down buildings, bury objects, and set fire to anything that will burn. However, most lava flows creep along slower than walking pace, and people can normally run or drive away from the danger of an approaching lava flow.

◀ A lava flow creeps along, engulfing and incinerating palm trees on Hawaii.

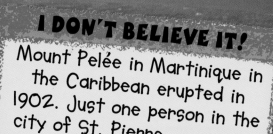
▲ This aerial view shows the paths of the pyroclastic flows that swept down Mount Unzen, Japan.

43 The deadliest volcano hazards are pyroclastic flows. Temperatures inside these high-speed avalanches of hot ash, gas, and rock reach hundreds of degrees Fahrenheit. When a pyroclastic flow hits objects such as trees or houses, the blast flattens them, and the heat burns them to a cinder.

44 Pyroclastic flows can travel as fast as a jet plane. Anyone caught in a pyroclastic flow cannot survive the heat. In 1991, hundreds of observers and journalists gathered at Mount Unzen, Japan, as it began to erupt. Forty-two of them were killed by a pyroclastic flow.

▲ These houses were buried by volcanic ash from an eruption on the island of Heimaey, Iceland, in 1973.

45 Volcanic ash is deadly. As ash falls down after an eruption, it is often still scorching hot. This can start fires and, if breathed in, can cause suffocation. A layer of volcanic ash just an inch or two thick can make the roof of a house collapse.

Side effects

46 Volcanoes can set off floods, mudflows, and tsunamis. It is not just the material expelled by volcanoes, such as lava, bombs, ash, and pyroclastic flows that is dangerous. Eruptions can also cause hazardous side effects, which are just as deadly.

47 A volcanic mudflow is a river of ash and water. Mudflows are also called lahars. Some occur when hot ash falls on snow and ice on the upper slopes of volcanoes. Ash mixes with the meltwater and flows downhill. Others form from heavy rain falling on the ash deposits. When a mudflow stops flowing, it sets solid, like concrete.

QUIZ

1. What is a lahar?
2. What town was buried by a mudflow in 1985?
3. What happens to tsunami waves as they hit shallow water?

Answers:
1. Lahar is another name for a volcanic mudflow 2. Armero in Colombia, South America 3. They increase in size and become closer together

▲ Near the crater of Mount Ruapehu in New Zealand, a mudflow, or lahar, begins to flow down the slopes. The flow formed after an eruption in 2007.

48 **The town of Armero, Colombia, was devastated by a mudflow.** In 1985, the volcano Nevado del Ruiz erupted. It was not a large eruption, but ash melted snow on the summit, setting off a mudflow. It rushed down a river valley and swept through Armero. Practically the entire population of 22,000 died.

▶ The remains of the town of Armero, Colombia, after it was buried by a mudflow.

49 **Volcanoes can cause floods.** Landslides set off by eruptions can fall into lakes, causing floods in rivers below. In Iceland, volcanoes sometimes erupt under the ice cap. The eruptions melt huge volumes of ice, setting off vast floods that sweep out to sea.

50 **Explosive eruptions can set off tsunamis.** A tsunami is a huge wave that travels across the sea and causes floods on any coasts it hits. The eruption of the volcanic island of Krakatoa, Indonesia, in 1883, set off tsunamis that traveled thousands of miles around the world.

▼ When Krakatoa erupted, nearby islands were swamped by tsunamis set off by pyroclastic flows entering the sea.

Pyroclastic flow enters the sea

Far-apart, shallow ripples travel across the sea

As the waves approach shallower water, they increase in size and become closer together

Using volcanoes

▲ Wairakei power plant in New Zealand is located on a field of geothermal activity. The pipes carry water heated by underground rocks.

51 **Millions of people live near active volcanoes.** About one in ten of all the people in the world could be in danger from eruptions. However, people living near volcanoes can benefit from them—heat from volcanoes can be turned into electricity, and the soil is good for farming.

52 **Volcanoes are sources of energy.** The rocks around them are normally extremely hot. Heat energy from the Earth, called geothermal energy, can be collected and used for heating and to generate electricity. At geothermal power plants, water is pumped down into the ground where it is heated, creating hot water and steam. The hot water is used to heat homes and the steam to drive turbines and generators.

53 **Sulfur is mined from around volcanoes.** This yellow mineral is an important raw material for the chemical industries. Sulfur crystals are common around the vents of volcanoes and hot springs because magma gives off sulfurous gases. Sulfur is also extracted from volcanic rocks.

54 **Volcanic soil is good for farming.** Soil is normally made up of broken-down rock. Near volcanoes, soil is made up of eroded lava or ash and is rich in the minerals that plants need to grow. Mayon, a volcano in the Phillipines, regularly erupts explosively, but the land around Mayon is still farmed.

55 **Many people believe water filtered through volcanic rock is good for your health.** Natural sources of water in volcanic regions are rich in minerals including calcium and magnesium, which are good for growth and general health. A lot of mineral water is bottled at its source and exported for sale.

▼ In 2006, 20,000 people were evacuated due to the eruption of Mayon, the most active volcano in the Phillipines.

◄ A miner collects pieces of sulfur at a crater in Indonesia. Huge deposits of sulfur can build up around a volcano's crater.

Volcano science

56 **The science of volcanoes is called volcanology.** Scientists called volcanologists study the structure of volcanoes, causes of eruptions, old lava flows, and how ash travels in the air. They also monitor volcanoes to try to predict future eruptions.

▼ In 1994, the Dante II robot was lowered into the hot crater of Mount Spurr, Alaska. It collected gas and water samples and recorded video pictures.

▲ A volcanologist measures the levels of different gases coming from a fumarole.

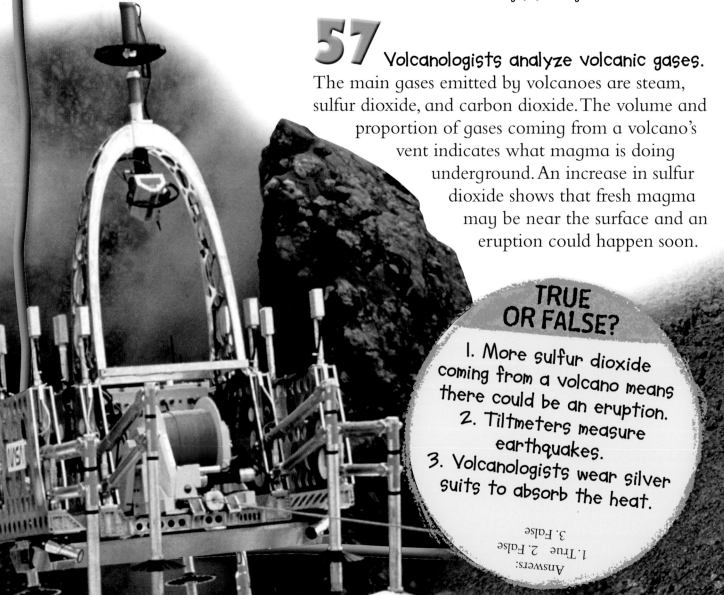

57 Volcanologists analyze volcanic gases. The main gases emitted by volcanoes are steam, sulfur dioxide, and carbon dioxide. The volume and proportion of gases coming from a volcano's vent indicates what magma is doing underground. An increase in sulfur dioxide shows that fresh magma may be near the surface and an eruption could happen soon.

TRUE OR FALSE?

1. More sulfur dioxide coming from a volcano means there could be an eruption.
2. Tiltmeters measure earthquakes.
3. Volcanologists wear silver suits to absorb the heat.

Answers:
1. True 2. False 3. False

58 **Earthquakes show that magma is moving.** Volcanologists set up earthquake-detecting instruments called seismographs on volcanoes. If earthquakes become more frequent, an eruption may be about to happen. Tiltmeters are used to detect if the ground is bulging. This shows if magma is building up underneath.

▼ Heat-reflecting silver suits protect volcanologists measuring the temperature of lava at Fournaise volcano, Reunion Island.

59 **Volcanologists study old lava flows.** Evidence of previous eruptions is a good guide to what might happen in the future. Old lava flows and ashfall on and around a volcano show the frequency and size of past eruptions. This gives a good indication of the areas that might be affected by future eruptions.

60 **Volcanologists wear protective clothes.** Hot rocks, lava flows, bombs, falling ash, and poisonous gases make active volcanoes dangerous places to be. When they visit volcanoes, volcanologists wear sturdy boots, hard hats, and heat-resistant gloves. In very dangerous areas, they also wear heat-reflecting overalls and gas masks.

Fighting volcanoes

61 People cannot stop volcanoes from erupting. However, we can reduce the damage that volcanoes cause by stopping or diverting lava and mudflows away from cities and towns. Injury and death can also be prevented by predicting eruptions accurately.

▼ The towering lava flows destroyed many houses on the island of Heimaey, Iceland, during the eruption in 1973.

I DON'T BELIEVE IT!

Islanders of Heimaey pumped a total of 222.4 million cubic feet of seawater (enough to fill 2,000 Olympic-sized swimming pools) onto the lava to stop it.

62 A lava flow was stopped with seawater. In 1973, an eruption on the island of Heimaey, Iceland, sent lava flows heading toward the island's harbor, where its fishing fleet was moored. Islanders pumped seawater onto the lava for months. Eventually it was stopped, and the harbor was saved.

◄ During the eruption of Mount Etna, Italy, in 1983, bulldozers piled up rock in banks to channel a lava flow away from houses.

64 There are various ways to reduce the damage of lava flows. In the past, people have built walls and dug channels to divert flows. Bombs have also been dropped on lava flows to make them spread out and slow down, as used on Mount Etna in 1992.

63 Mudflows can be reduced with dams. Deadly mudflows are fast-flowing and dense with ash and heavy debris. Special dams, called sabo dams, slow mudflows by trapping the ash and debris and letting the water flow harmlessly away.

65 Preparation saves lives. People living in danger zones near active volcanoes have a plan of action in case of eruption. Local authorities should also communicate with volcanologists and the emergency services when an eruption threatens so that people can be evacuated in good time.

▶ Sabo dams on the slopes of Sakurajima volcano in Japan are designed to slow mudflows.

Mount St. Helens

66 Mount St. Helens erupted in 1980. It is part of a range of volcanoes in western North America called the Cascades. The eruption of Mount St. Helens was one of the most explosive and spectacular ever seen.

▲ Mount St. Helens before the 1980 eruption. The bulge that grew on the north side is clearly visible.

67 Mount St. Helens bulged outward before the blast. The eruption began in March 1980 with a cloud of ash that grew to nearly 4 miles tall. In April, the north side of the volcano began bulging outward. Gradually the bulge grew, showing that magma was building up underneath.

▶ Ash blasting from the vent of Mount St. Helens during the eruption. The cloud grew more than 12 miles high.

▶ The scars of the devastating mudflows and pyroclastic flows can still be seen in this satellite image taken in 1997.

68
The bulge collapsed on May 18. The pressure on the magma was released suddenly, and the volcano exploded sideways. A pyroclastic flow hurtled across the landscape at more than 186 miles per hour. It flattened millions of trees, some 20 miles away. Landslides of rock, mixed with water, snow, and ice, caused mudflows that traveled nearly 19 miles away.

▼ The gaping hole blown in the north side of Mount St. Helens.

69
Fifty-seven people were killed at Mount St. Helens. They were forestry workers, volcanologists, campers, and tourists. Most victims thought they were a safe distance away from the volcano. However, nobody expected the devastating sideways blast.

70
Mount St. Helens is rebuilding itself. Nearly 1,000 feet was blown off the top of the volcano in the 1980 eruption. Since then, a new lava dome (heap of solidified lava) has grown inside the crater, a sign that one day Mount St. Helens will erupt again.

I DON'T BELIEVE IT!
Local man Harry Truman refused to leave his home near Mount St. Helens despite warnings. The lodge he lived in was buried in the eruption.

35

Mount Pinatubo

71 Mount Pinatubo erupted violently in June 1991. It is a stratovolcano in the Philippines, close to the city of Manila. Its 1991 eruption was the most devastating of the 20th century.

72 Mount Pinatubo had been dormant for 600 years. The first signs of an eruption were explosions of steam from the summit. Volcanologists from the Philippines and United States quickly set up an observatory at the nearby Clark Air Base to monitor the activity. They set up instruments on the volcano that showed magma was on the move below.

73 An exclusion zone was set up around the volcano. At first, the zone extended 6 miles from the volcano. This was steadily increased to 20 miles. In total, 58,000 people were evacuated, which saved many lives.

▼ A truck races to escape a boiling pyroclastic flow rolling down from Mount Pinatubo.

▲ Ash fell far from the eruption column of Mount Pinatubo, smothering local villages and countryside.

74 **Mount Pinatubo erupted with giant explosions.** An ash cloud rose 25 miles into the sky, and pyroclastic flows reached up to 12.6 miles from the volcano. They deposited ash and debris hundreds of feet deep along their route. Ash in the air made it dark in the middle of the day and gases from the eruption spread around the Earth. This caused temperatures to fall by 0.9°F for several months.

▶ A false-color satellite image taken after Pinatubo's eruption shows mudflows in red and the large crater (center) left after the eruption.

75 **Heavy rains caused devastating mudflows.** A typhoon hit the Philippines as Mount Pinatubo erupted, bringing days of torrential rain. The rain set off huge mudflows that swept away thousands of homes and 38.6 square miles of valuable farmland. More mudflows followed as the heavy rains returned in the following years.

Mount Vesuvius

76 Mount Vesuvius, Italy, is the only active volcano on mainland Europe. In A.D. 79, when Italy was ruled by the ancient Romans, Mount Vesuvius erupted violently.

77 The eruption was seen by a Roman named Pliny the Younger. Pliny wrote letters describing the ash cloud—he said it looked like a giant pine tree. His uncle, Pliny the Elder, went to help people escape, but was killed by falling ash. Today, explosive eruptions are called Plinian eruptions after Pliny.

▶ Ash and pyroclasts raining down from Vesuvius would have caused complete panic in the streets of Pompeii.

78 The city of Pompeii was completely buried by ash. Pompeii lay 9 miles south of Mount Vesuvius. Ash and pumice rained down on the city, filling the streets and making buildings collapse.

I DON'T BELIEVE IT!

Before A.D. 79, Mount Vesuvius had not erupted for 800 years. The Romans did not realize it was a volcano or that there was any danger.

▲ The last major eruption of Mount Vesuvius happened in 1944. Two villages on the slopes were hit by lava flows.

79 **People had little time to escape.** Thousands died as they ran through the streets, suffocated by the hot, choking ash. Since excavations started in the 1750s, archeologists digging through the layers of ash have uncovered the remains of people and animals.

80 **Mount Vesuvius is still a dangerous volcano.** It has erupted dozens of times since A.D. 79. Nearby towns and villages have been regularly destroyed by eruptions, yet millions of people still live close to the volcano.

Volcanoes at sea

81 **Many islands are the tops of volcanoes.** Volcanic islands grow over hot spots and other regions of volcanic activity under the sea. There are hundreds of hidden undersea volcanoes that have not broken the ocean's surface yet. These are called seamounts.

▲ Anak Krakatoa is a new island in Indonesia that first appeared out of the sea in 1927. It has grown in the place of the island of Krakatoa.

82 **Underwater eruptions produce pillow lava.** As lava is exposed to cold sea water, it cools quickly, forming round humps of lava that look like pillows piled on top of each other. Pillow lava also forms when lava flows reach the sea.

TRUE OR FALSE?

1. Mauna Kea is the world's tallest mountain.
2. More Hawaiian islands will form in the future.
3. Surtsey island is near Fiji.

Answers:
1. True—from the sea floor, Mauna Kea is slightly taller than Mount Everest 2. True—as the tectonic plate moves over the hot spot more islands will form 3. False—Surtsey is near Iceland. The island that formed in 2006 is near Fiji.

40

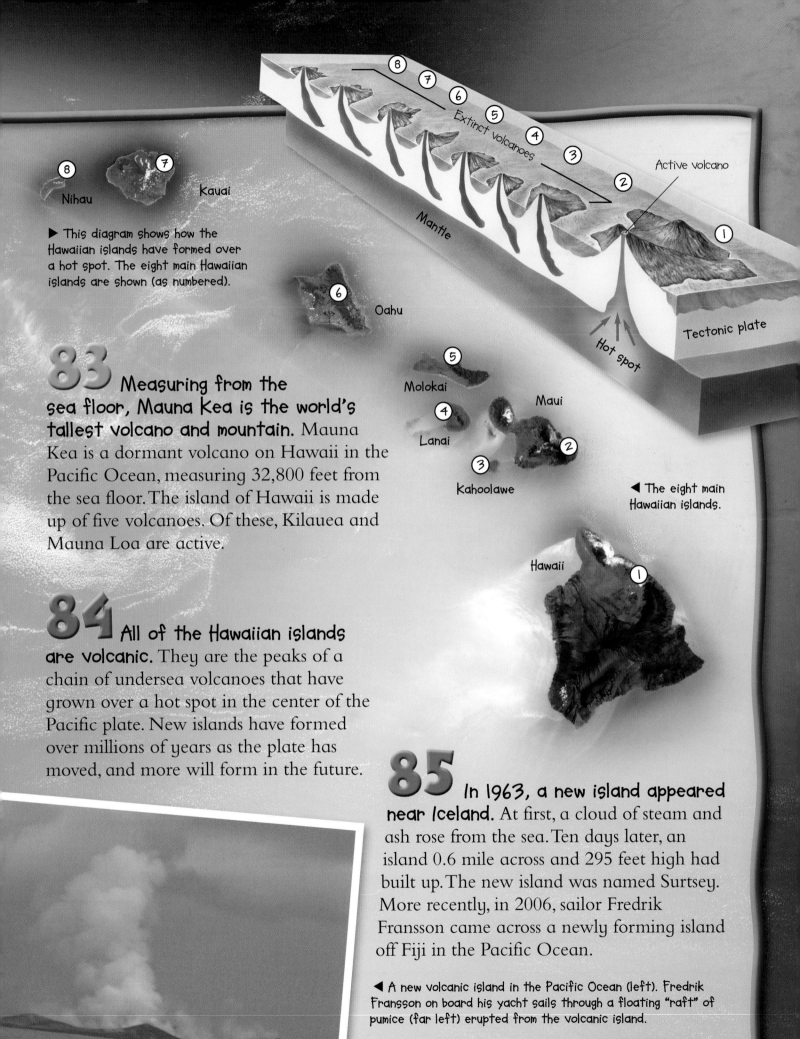

8

7

Nihau

Kauai

8

7

6

5

4

3

2

1

Extinct volcanoes

Active volcano

Mantle

Hot spot

Tectonic plate

▶ This diagram shows how the Hawaiian islands have formed over a hot spot. The eight main Hawaiian islands are shown (as numbered).

6

Oahu

5

Molokai

4

Lanai

Maui

2

3

Kahoolawe

◀ The eight main Hawaiian islands.

Hawaii

1

83 **Measuring from the sea floor, Mauna Kea is the world's tallest volcano and mountain.** Mauna Kea is a dormant volcano on Hawaii in the Pacific Ocean, measuring 32,800 feet from the sea floor. The island of Hawaii is made up of five volcanoes. Of these, Kilauea and Mauna Loa are active.

84 **All of the Hawaiian islands are volcanic.** They are the peaks of a chain of undersea volcanoes that have grown over a hot spot in the center of the Pacific plate. New islands have formed over millions of years as the plate has moved, and more will form in the future.

85 **In 1963, a new island appeared near Iceland.** At first, a cloud of steam and ash rose from the sea. Ten days later, an island 0.6 mile across and 295 feet high had built up. The new island was named Surtsey. More recently, in 2006, sailor Fredrik Fransson came across a newly forming island off Fiji in the Pacific Ocean.

◀ A new volcanic island in the Pacific Ocean (left). Fredrik Fransson on board his yacht sails through a floating "raft" of pumice (far left) erupted from the volcanic island.

41

The biggest volcanoes

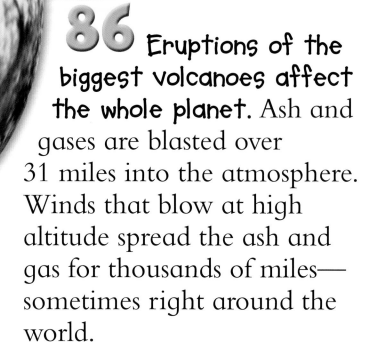

86 **Eruptions of the biggest volcanoes affect the whole planet.** Ash and gases are blasted over 31 miles into the atmosphere. Winds that blow at high altitude spread the ash and gas for thousands of miles—sometimes right around the world.

VEI 8—Mega-colossal
Ash column height 25 km +
Volume erupted 1,000 km³

VEI 7—Super-colossal
Ash column height 25 km +
Volume erupted 100 km³

VEI 6—Colossal
Ash column height 25 km +
Volume erupted 10 km³

VEI 5—Paroxysmal
Ash column height 25 km +
Volume erupted 1 km³

VEI 4—Cataclysmic
Ash column height 10–25 km
Volume erupted 100,000,000 m³

VEI 3—Severe
Ash column height 3–15 km
Volume erupted 10,000,000 m³

VEI 2—Explosive
Ash column height 1–5 km
Volume erupted 1,000,000 m³

VEI 1—Gentle
Ash column height 100–1000 m
Volume erupted 10,000 m³

▲ The Volcanic Explosivity Index. Each stage represents a tenfold increase in explosivity.

87 **The power of an eruption is measured on the VEI scale.** VEI stands for Volcanic Explosivity Index and it is based on the amount of material erupted and the height of the ash column. Each stage on the scale has a name—1 is a "gentle" eruption and 8 is "mega-colossal." The eruption of Mount St. Helens had a VEI of 5 and Mount Vesuvius in A.D. 79 had a VEI of 4.

88 **The biggest eruption in historical time had a VEI of 7.** In 1815, the Indonesian volcano Tambora erupted. Ash spread around the world. It blocked sunlight and caused temperatures to fall and crops to fail. The following year, 1816, is known as "the year without a summer" because of the cold weather. Over 90,000 people were killed by the eruption.

Before the 1883 eruption

Today

Anak Krakatoa

89

The island of Krakatoa was destroyed in an eruption. Krakatoa was a volcanic island in Indonesia. In 1883, it erupted in a series of huge explosions that blew the island apart. The eruption caused tsunamis that devastated nearby islands and coasts. Today, a new volcano—Anak Krakatoa (meaning "child of Krakatoa")—is growing in the sea where Krakatoa once stood.

▲ An artist's impression of the eruption of Krakatoa in 1883 (main image). Most of the island was destroyed during the eruption (above right).

90

The eruption of Toba had a VEI of 8. Toba in Indonesia erupted about 74,000 years ago. Volcanologists think it was the biggest eruption in the last two million years. Its effects may have nearly wiped out the human population. Eruptions of this massive scale are called super-eruptions.

◄ The 62-mile-long Lake Toba fills the caldera left by the super-eruption of Toba.

QUIZ

1. What does VEI stand for?
2. What does the name Anak Krakatoa mean?
3. Which volcanic eruption had a VEI of 8?

Answers:
1. Volcanic Explosivity Index 2. Child of Krakatoa 3. Toba, 74,000 years ago

Past and future

91 **The Earth was once covered by volcanoes.** When the Earth formed 4,500 billion years ago, its surface was molten. It gradually cooled and a crust formed. At this time, the Earth's surface was covered with millions of volcanoes.

▶ The young planet Earth was a fiery ball of molten rock.

92 A VEI 8 eruption happens roughly once every 100,000 years. That is what volcanologists think as an average. A VEI 8 eruption would wipe out many countries and kill off much of the world's human population.

▲ Billions of years ago, soon after the Earth was formed, the surface was covered with volcanoes.

I DON'T BELIEVE IT!

There are volcanoes on Io, one of Jupiter's moons. They erupt giant fountains of sulfur that make the surface appear yellow.

93 We do not know when the next super-volcano will erupt. Super-eruptions are at the highest end (and beyond) of the VEI scale. The last super-eruption was Toba 74,000 years ago. The next one could happen in tens of thousands of years, more than a million years, or even much sooner!

▶ Olympus Mons on Mars photographed from overhead by a space probe.

94 Yellowstone National Park could erupt soon!
Yellowstone is over a hot spot in the crust. It is the site of a caldera that is 37 miles across. There were VEI 8 eruptions here 2 million, 1.3 million, and 640,000 years ago. That means another one is due.

95 Other planets have volcanoes, too. Astronomers have discovered more than 1,000 volcanoes on Venus, but all are extinct. Mars has the largest volcano in the Solar System, called Olympus Mons, which is 15 miles high.

◀ Tourists flock to Yellowstone National Park to see the volcanic features, such as the Old Faithful geyser. The park lies on the site of a super-volcano.

Myths and legends

96 **People once thought eruptions were the work of gods.** Until scientists began to understand volcanoes, nobody knew how or why they erupted. People were scared by eruptions and thought that they meant the gods were angry.

▲ The word "volcano" originates from Vulcan, the Roman god of fire.

97 **Vulcan was the Roman god of fire.** Roman legend says that Vulcan lived on the island of Vulcano, near Sicily. He was blacksmith to the gods, forging their weapons. Fire and smoke from Vulcano were thought to be caused by Vulcan hammering hot metal in his forge.

98 **Mount Fuji in Japan is a sacred mountain.** For hundreds of years, Japanese people have made pilgrimages to its summit. Mount Fuji is one of the world's most beautiful volcanoes, with a perfect snow-capped cone and lakes around its lower slopes. It appears many times in Japanese art and photography and is also shown on Japanese currency.

QUIZ

1. What was Vulcan the Roman god of?
2. Where was the goddess Pele thought to live?
3. What did the gods turn Popocatépetl and his princess into?

Answers:
1. Fire 2. Kilauea on Hawaii 3. Mountains

99 Pele is the Hawaiian goddess of volcanoes.
Hawaiians believe that Pele lives on Kilauea on Hawaii. Drop-shaped pieces of volcanic glass erupted from Hawaiian voclanoes are known as Pele's tears, and thin strands of the same material are called Pele's hair.

▼ The perfect cone of Mount Fuji. The mountain is sacred for many Japanese people.

▲ Pele, the Hawaiian goddess of volcanoes, is also goddess of fire and lightning.

100 A warrior was named after the Mexican volcano Popocatépetl.
In Aztec folklore, the warrior Popocatépetl fell in love with a princess. They wanted to marry, but the princess's father would only agree if Popocatépetl went to battle for him. He was away for such a long time that the princess thought he was dead, so she drank poison and died. When Popocatépetl returned, he held the princess in his arms, and it is said the gods turned them both into mountains. Popocatépetl made fire because of his anger.

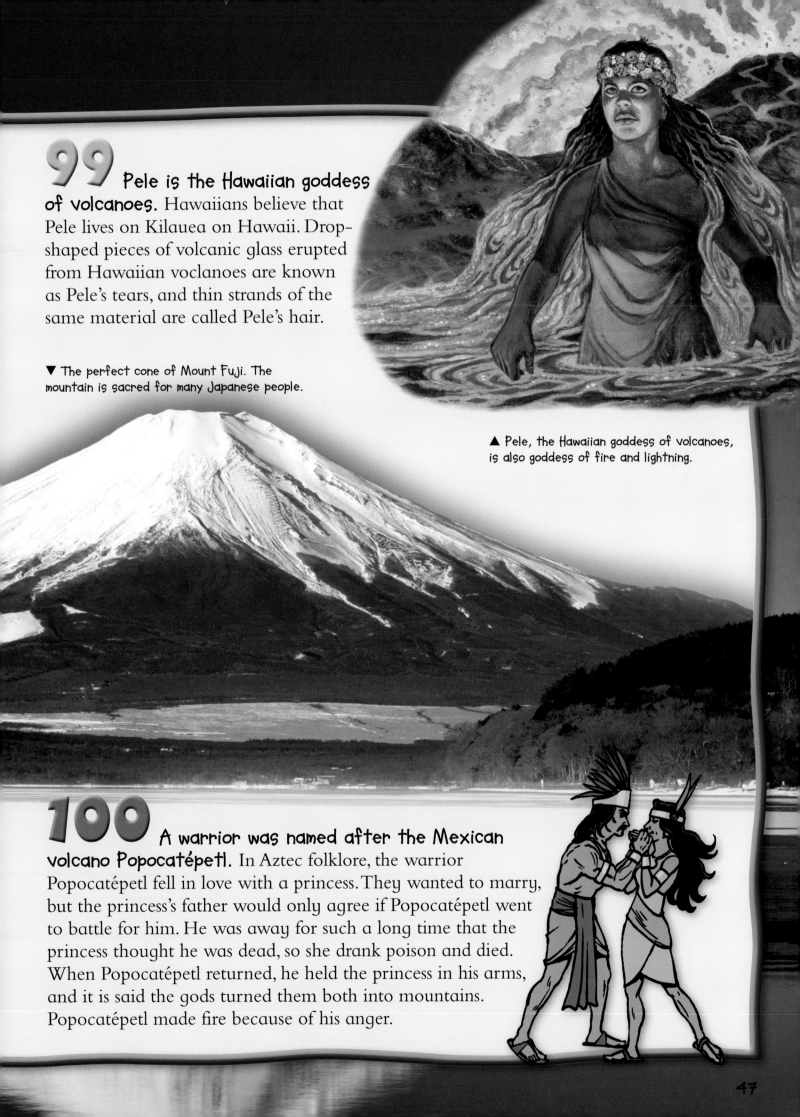

47

Index

Entries in **bold** refer to main subject entries. Entries in *italics* refer to illustrations.